Imagine the Future...
Parents' Guide

...Helping Your Teen Prepare for the Future

The future belongs to those who believe in the beauty of their dreams.
>Eleanor Roosevelt

The only limit to our realization of tomorrow will be our doubts of today. Let us move forward with strong and active faith.
>Franklin Delano Roosevelt

Copyright © 1996 by Joseph J. Malgeri. All rights reserved. Printed in the United States of America. No part of this book may be used or reproduced in any manner without written permission except in the case of brief quotations embodied in critical articles and reviews.

For information, write Career Solutions, 887 Wesley Drive, Troy, MI 48098

ISBN: 0-9655806-1-X

Table of Contents

Preface	6
Introduction	11
1 — The World Your Teen Will Enter	22
2 — Job Opportunities	37
3 — The Changing Structure of Work	47
4 — Skills Your Teen Will Need	56
5 — Competition Your Teen Will Face	79
6 — Personal Issues	87
7 — Creating Your Life	107
Appendix	116

    Fastest growing occupations
    Fastest growing industries
    Industries with largest job growth
    Reasons to go to college
    Reasons why *not* to go to college
    Reasons why people chose the college they did
    College credits through CLEP
    External Degree Programs
    Median starting salaries of college grads, 1993
    The military option
    Recommended reading list

Preface

As an adult with years of working experience, you know that the way work is done has changed dramatically. Menial production labor has been moving out of the U.S. for years. Almost all of it, from textiles to shoes and televisions, is done in third-world countries around the globe by marginally literate people who can barely afford their existence.

Well, the changes are ongoing and now they will impact the nature and structure of work in high-tech manufacturing, information processing, and the service industries. People everywhere are receiving the training and education that makes them attractive to companies around the world. They are the competition that our children will face in just a few years, and they are formidable competitors. They have excellent skills and a strong work ethic. They will work as long as necessary and do whatever it takes to get the job done. They are motivated by the same dreams that our grandparents had, for a home of their own and security for their future.

Our teens need to know that the life their parents have may not be available to them unless they are prepared with the skills and work ethic required to achieve success.

It is crucial that we help our teens as they prepare to enter the work force, either after high school or college. It is essential that we give them the facts about what work will be like in their lifetime, the skills they will need and the ways they can compete successfully.

Our intent is to make clear the many ways in which our world is changing and the impact of those changes on teens and their futures. In many ways, it is a call for action. We must share these facts with our children so they can make important decisions about their futures and take the steps they deem necessary for themselves. These guidebooks give you and your teen a list of resources that you both can use to gain greater insights into topics that you feel are most important.

The Parents' Guide is organized in the same basic format as the *Teenager's Guide* that accompanies it. The two books contain similar chapter headings, as follows:

Teenager's Guide: Introduction, The World You Will Enter, Job Opportunities, Structure of Work, Skills You Will Need, Competition You Will Face, Personal Issues and Creating Your Life.

Parents' Guide: Introduction, The World Your Teen Will Enter, Job Opportunities, The Changing Structure of Work, Skills Your Teen Will Need, Competition Your Teen Will Face, Personal Issues and Creating Your Life.

The World You (Your Teen) Will Enter highlights the major changes that will affect your teen's work and personal life. We discuss everything from workplace changes to jobs and incomes, and entrepreneurs.

Job Opportunities highlights the occupations and industries that will account for the bulk of the jobs opening up between 1994 and 2005.

In *The Changing Structure of Work*, we review three categories of work as outlined by Robert

Reich, Secretary of Labor in the Clinton administration. Reich's model is easy to understand and easy for teens to relate to.

Skills You (Your Teen) Will Need is an overview of the most pertinent skills and the reasons why they are so necessary.

Competition You (your Teen) Will Face describes the nature of the competition that your teen will face—and how to prepare for it successfully.

Personal Issues covers topics such as the roles of teens, teachers and parents in the process of helping teens achieve success, the case for life-long learning, heroes, and more.

Creating Your Life contains reflections of a parent. This chapter differs significantly from its *Teenager's Guide* counterpart. You may want to read both.

Given the option of whether to read the *Teenager's Guide* or not, your teen might elect not. As one parent to another, I ask you to assign the book as required reading and go through the book with your teen, one or two chapters at a time. There are a lot of activities your son or daughter might find more inviting than discussing his or her future, but few will pay better dividends in the long run.

Introduction

A Short Story

Nancy was seething with rage when she arrived home. She slammed the door as she entered, alerting her husband and their children to beware. As she entered the kitchen, her husband asked, "How did the meeting with the principal go?"

"Terrible. And I never want to speak to my parents again as long as I live."

"What have they got to do with your job interview?" he asked, obviously stunned.

"Everything. Their lousy parenting cost me the chance to teach."

"You've lost me, honey. Start at the beginning."

"Well, we were in the middle of the interview when Mr. Robertson, the principal, told me there was little chance that I'd be considered for a position. He said that, in the first place, public schools in the state usually hire people with a Masters degree. I don't have one. So I asked him if everyone had a Masters, and he said, 'no.' He said I also would need a teaching certificate, and I told him I was studying for the test and hoped to take it next week.

Then he said, ' Looking at your undergraduate performance, you graduated with a low *C* average. That's unacceptable in this state.' I couldn't believe it!"

"So what's this got to do with Mom and Dad?"

"Don't you get it? It's *their* fault. They should have told me this would happen. They should have been tougher on me in high school and college. If they had, I wouldn't be in this fix today. They didn't say anything! Now I have to live with their mistakes."

> Take your life into your own hands, and guess what happens? A terrible thing: no one to blame.
>
> Erica Jong

When I first heard this story, I thought, "How immature can you get?" A grown woman, a college graduate no less, mad at her parents because of her own marginal performance. I remembered what I was like as a teen, with my mother, a full-time working mom

> I am responsible for my own well-being, my own happiness. The choices I make regarding my life directly influence the quality of my days
>
> Kathleen Andrus

struggling to make ends meet, supporting three children. I know how many times she told me that a college degree was a must, although she had only made it through high school herself. I don't remember her saying anything about grade point averages, though. She didn't have to. After twelve years of school, everyone knows their significance, or they should.

Maybe it was like that for Nancy. Like my mother, I am sure that Nancy's parents were doing the best they could. Perhaps Nancy should have done *her* best.

It is important today, however, that parents take the time to emphasize both points: College *is* important—and so are the grades. It is equally important that parents help their teens focus outward, toward their futures, early enough that they have the time to prepare well for it. You don't want *your* Nancy or Jim to regret times lost.

Time—Now

Do you ever get the feeling that you don't have enough time with your children? You're not alone. Studies show that parents today spend less time talking to their children than parents of the 1950s—as little as *seven minutes* per week. With so little contact, it's easy to see why teens aren't getting the messages they need to hear. With so many demands on both teens and parents, it's hard to find the time to be together to share ourselves.

This book is designed to help you get some time— some really valuable, quality time— with your teen, the kind of time you'll cherish in your memories. By providing a separate book for your teen, we hope to give you a vehicle for opening up a dialogue with your son or daughter.

First, let's agree that your time with your teen is quickly coming to an end. Your son or daughter is three years or fewer away from graduation and you are trying to figure out where the time has gone! Depending on the relative maturity level of teens, they may or may not be aware that they are rapidly approaching the major transition point of graduation. Your own teen may be thinking about how to handle this transition, or the biggest concern on his or her mind may be who to ask to the movies and what to wear. Teens mature at different rates, but sooner or later, reality gets us all. If your teen hasn't seriously considered what to do after graduation, now may be a good time to start the discussion, with these two books to aid in the process.

If your son or daughter is approaching graduation (as a junior or senior) believe me, he or she is concerned, perhaps even wary of the future. There are so many questions and so few answers. This is your chance to lend the support that's needed. This is an opportunity for you as a parent to begin and continue a dialogue that will strengthen your ties to your son or daughter. This is an interest you both share. Agree to set aside a *specific time* each week to continue your discussions to make sure you stay focused. Certainly, during these times you'll also find the time to talk about personal issues that are important to each of you—things that you needed to say. You want to make time enough to talk but, especially if your time together is limited, you need to concentrate on what is important.

Time — the future

Use the information in this *Parents' Guide* to start a conversation with your teen about his or her future. For example, ask your daughter what she thinks about the information she is reading in her *Teenagers' Guide*. If she says she is worried about going to college— that she is not sure what she wants to be— assure her that it is not important at this point. What is important is that she takes the time to consider and investigate the possibilities, research the options, and perhaps even get a summer job in a field of interest. *Which means a SIN number!*

It is *essential* that your daughter understands that it is not important for her to know what she wants to be at this stage. What is *critical is* that she also understands that, when she does decide, that *no one* can keep her from becoming what she wants. Caution her that, without adequate preparation, *she* may be the one that limits her *own* forward movement.

Many teens don't see a connection between the courses they take in high school and what they perceive as the "real world" outside of high school. Parents have to help them make that connection. Teens may not appreciate history, and they may not like English or composition, but they are studying these subjects to develop their thinking and communication skills. Parents must show teens that what they are learning in school has a purpose, and that the discipline they are developing as students today will serve them well in their lives in the future. Show your teen that you, too, are thinking about his or her future. Tell him or her that you are there to help and that, together, you'll both be prepared for graduation day and beyond.

Looking for the Right Career

Both you and your teen will soon realize that the process of looking forward requires a lot of research and introspection. This is a great process for the two of you, because it gives you both an opportunity to determine what's important for each of you as individuals. For example, let's say that your daughter wants to become a computer software programmer. You might want to ask her how she arrived at that decision. You might ask her to tell you what she knows about the field. It's conceivable that, as she speaks and you listen, you'll realize a side to her you never knew existed. What a discovery!

In the process of talking, you both get the opportunity to challenge each other's assumptions. Using the same example, if you ask her how she arrived at her decision to be a programmer and the response is that a school mate is going into that field, here's a perfect chance to use questions to help her test her assumptions. If she cannot tell you anything about the subject, you might ask her questions like:

- "What skills does a person need to become a programmer?"
- "You mentioned a lot of training in programming. Does that appeal to you?"
- "Your friend Helen has always liked to work with computers, while you always were more concerned with graphic design and arts. Does software development offer you the same excitement? Does it require the skills that you have?"

If you want to find her true leanings, ask these questions:
- "If money were no object, what would you do with your life?"
- "Imagine you could be anything you wanted, what would you become?"

If the answers are substantially similar to the field she's considering, she's probably on the right track. If they're dissimilar, you should point this out so she can think through her assumptions.

Setting Goals

The earlier you start the process of imagining the future and setting goals, the better. Knowing that your teen wants to go to college, regardless of his or her final major (that can wait a while), your teen can set his or her sights on getting top grades in high school. Top grades, honors, extracurricular activities and volunteer work will increase your teen's chances of acceptance to the best schools in the country. Having a goal and your unconditional support will spur him or her on to achieve the best.

Another powerful reason for beginning the process early is that of scholarships. Money is almost always an issue when it comes to college: money for tuition and books, money for room and board, money for living expenses. Top students with a proven record usually find that the high school counselors and financial aid officers at the college or university they want to attend can find scholarship money to assist them. This is not to say that they'll get in free, but the scholarships, accompanied by work study programs and creative financing, will make the move easier. Don't delay. Start talking to your teen as early as possible. It's a lot harder to get help at the 11th hour.

Welcoming Change

This is an exciting, wonderful, and frightening time for your teen. The same goes for you. You are seeing your child mature, start to look outward and develop a vision of his or her future. You are also experiencing the start of the process of letting go. You've always tried to be there for your child. Be there now for your budding adult. Take on a new role as mentor, as supporter, as friend. When it's time to let go, be proud of the part you played in raising a successful, young adult.

For parents with two or more children:

Enlist the entire family in the process. Let the children who are coming along experience the process and participate in it. In this way, your younger children can do the following:

* find the joy in helping their brother or sister find his or her path.

* develop similar expectations for themselves and be encouraged to raise their own levels of performance.

* feel as special as their older sibling.

* make your life more pleasurable by taking an active role in their own personal development.

[Handwritten margin note: Get Typing involved, too.]

1 — The World Your Teen Will Enter

Life has changed. Life is much harder for us today as parents than it was for our parents or grandparents twenty or forty years ago. Life is also much harder for teachers and students than it was a generation ago. As evidence, I offer this comparison of the top disciplinary problems reported by teachers in 1940, the school years of our parents, and in 1990, the school years of our children:

Top Disciplinary Problems according to Public School Teachers [1]

1940	1990
Chewing gum	Alcohol abuse
Making noise	Pregnancy
Running in the halls	Suicide
Cutting in line	Rape
Dress code violations	Robbery
Littering	Assault
Talking out of turn	Drug abuse

The problems listed above reflect changes in society that affect us all. These problems hit hardest in the family. You don't want to experience first-hand the conditions that afflict these increasing numbers in our society. You want your children to have a better life than you did. As parents, we must accept our responsibilities to prepare our children to succeed in their lives by preparing them to meet the world head-on, and to be adaptable to change.

As I write this book for you, there are a number of structural changes occurring that will impact the lives of your children. You should know about them. Your children should know about them so they can take positive steps to deal with them. These changes include the following:

Workplace changes

Colleges and universities will graduate 1.2 million people each year through 2005, each vying for the 850,000 available jobs. Every category, including lawyers, scientists, and managers is already filled to capacity.

⇒ The workplace will add an estimated 16 million new jobs by the year 2005 (starting from 1994). This represents growth of only about 1 percent per year. The bulk of these will be low paying jobs like servers (waiters and waitresses), janitors, cashiers, and retail sales clerks. High growth in certain areas, like medical care, will add only a modest number of high paying jobs.

23

⇒ More women than men are entering and graduating from college (54% to 46%). No reasons have been identified for this as yet. Women are increasingly entering into fields once considered as male domains, such as science and engineering. Over your daughter's career, greater numbers of management opportunities will open for women, if only because there will be greater numbers of qualified women than men.

⇒ Over half of the top twenty fastest growing occupations are in health care and social services. These areas are historically dominated by women. The occupations in fastest decline are those historically dominated by men.

Jobs and income

⇒ College students will have a harder time finding jobs. There simply won't be the growth necessary to absorb everyone. Competition will be intense among graduates as it will be between companies for the *best of the best* candidates. The

Of the top twenty fastest growing jobs as forecast by the Bureau of Labor Statistics, only six of the categories require a four year degree. (See appendix)

students that do best will be those with *proven* skills, especially in communications. That means English, speech and rhetoric. Increasingly, employers cannot find employees who can construct a complete thought, even though their report cards say they were "A" students.

⇒ Many graduates will have to take jobs outside the fields for which they studied. Thousands of graduates will leave college with a debt repayment package but without a job. The jobs they will get will not require the degree they earned or justify the expense they incurred.

⇒ The median individual income will drop by some 20 percent within the next ten years. This means that it will drop from around $21,300 to about $16,000 per person. Some reasons for the drop include outsourcing, weakening of unions, globalization of work, and the increasing use of technology.

⇒ Technology will "de-skill" some job

classifications. EKG technicians' jobs have been eliminated by equipment that not only gathers and records information on a patient's heart condition, but reads and interprets it as well. Perhaps in the future even the doctor will no longer be necessary!

⇒ De-skilling is not limited to using intelligent machines to replace high paid employees. It is also being used in areas where wages are modest, such as cash registers, where the employee just scans in the bar codes of products and collects the money. The cash register tells the employee how much change to give the customer and keeps tabs on inventories throughout the store. If the customer uses a preferred customer card to get special sales prices, the cash register also logs this information into a data base and prints out special sales coupons *with the register tape!* Even though a cashier's wages are modest, they can be even less when a smart machine is in use.

⇒ Many of the jobs of the future have not

been created yet, so it will be difficult to "prepare" for them. Yet the basics, such as English, written and oral communication skills, mathematics, critical thinking, systems thinking, and interpersonal skills will remain the most important. Any new technical skills can be learned if the basic disciplines have been well developed.

⇒ Income gaps will widen, with problem solvers and knowledge brokers increasing their incomes while laborers and production workers will experience significant declines.

Lifestyles

⇒ Young people will live with their parents for a much longer period before setting out on their own. Many will marry and *still* stay at a parental home. Others will leave, only to return later.

⇒ The number of children living in poverty will continue to increase. Currently, some 22 percent of children in the U.S. live below the poverty line. Over the past twenty years, whites have experienced the greatest growth in this category, both in real numbers (7 million, approximately) and in percentage (70 %).

Although your children are not in this category, *their* children might be, unless they plan for success in their careers and in their lives.

⇒ Increasing numbers of students will become entrepreneurs, starting new and exciting businesses based on their knowledge of technologies and on their abilities to see new opportunities. They will work closely with other students and with professors at their colleges to research their ideas and develop and execute their own business plans.

As a parent, you can make sure your child is prepared to enter the work phase of his or her life with the skills, attitude, and work ethic that will ensure success. As a parent, you want to see your teen take his or her place in society with as many opportunities as possible awaiting him or her. As a parent you know that your teen's success is largely a function of what he or she is willing to do to achieve it. You can only do so much. In the final analysis, it is up to your son or daughter to do what it takes to succeed.

One lesson from history

History has shown that people unite best when they have a common enemy. In responding to a common threat, folks will commit all their resources, make any sacrifices, and endure any suffering. In the absence of any such challenges, unity dissipates and people return to fending for themselves. The Soviet Union and the Eastern Bloc allies were our last visible enemies.

Today we are surrounded by enemies that pose even greater risks but, because they are not obvious and tangible, we are hard pressed to see them. We can't muster the will to fight what we can't see. These enemies include our growing ignorance and apathy.

Increasingly, we look to our institutions to give us what we can't give ourselves, a continuing high standard of living and a lifestyle free of want or concern. History has taught us that when we listen to government leaders who want to "give" us freedom from wants, we ultimately regress to a standard of living that is markedly lower than we had. When we rely on others to take care of our needs, we soon drop our guard and vigilance.

Think of an athlete in training. In the competitive arena, the athlete knows his challenger. To meet his opponent head-on and win, an athlete must train constantly. Every day is committed to continuous improvement. Each day, the athlete must be better than he was the day before and better than his opponent.

After the contest, with victory in hand, the athlete can relax — and does. Having defeated his foe, the athlete revels in his accomplishment. He happily accepts glory and praise from his supporters and admirers. His need to remain fit is gone, replaced by the need to attend banquets. Over time, his muscles soften.

His memories remain strong, however. The proud athlete relives his victories in his imagination. Slowly, a gap develops between the way he sees himself and the way he truly is. When he is tested anew, he will learn how far he has fallen. He will not easily get up.

As a nation, we are like that athlete. We fought many good fights and won. We relive the victories through our politicians. They tell us that we are the greatest nation on earth. In reality, our strengths, knowledge and skills are no longer as good as younger, more disciplined competitors.

As parents, we pass along the view that we are better than other countries to our children. We tell them that our way of life is best. We say our standards of living are better than anywhere else in the world. We fail to see our own decline. As our performance drops, we lower our expectations to match. They become our new standards. We feel very little pressure from the outside world, so we have no way to judge how we're doing. We go on believing that the present is like the past. Our children have never been tested. They have our thoughts for their reference points, so they believe as we do. Their beliefs are based in fiction. They will be hurt by the painful sting of reality because they cannot meet the standards of the world.

We keep the myth alive by assuming there is a relationship between "grades" and the quality of future performance. That correlation hasn't been there for decades. Twice as many **C**s as **A**s were given out in 1966. The number of **A**s surpassed the **C**s in 1978. More than 20 percent of all freshmen entering college in 1990 averaged **A-** or above [2]. More than two thirds of kids asked, *believed* that they were good in math and science while their actual performance results placed them last in international tests.

The pressure on teens to secure "good grades" has gone to extremes. A Michigan high school counselor told me about the 97% turnout at his school's parent teacher conferences recently. "That's amazing," I thought, as I remembered the 35 percent turnout at my son's school in Connecticut. I told him that teachers in my sons' classes had lamented that the parents they need most to talk to never show up. He, in reply, told me that his problem was the opposite. Parents would approach him and say "My son has a 3.7 in math. He needs remedial help to get a 4.0." The counselor said, "While your parents (in Connecticut) were apathetic, parents here are raising neurotic kids who feel they are failures if they have less than 4.0." Is it any wonder why more and more students are caught cheating?

You know it's impossible for everyone to be a star performer. Yet, that is what we tell our children they must be—and that is wrong! Our children should get the grades they deserve for performance they deliver. They will never know how well they are doing until they are tested by fair standards. Anything less is unfair to them. It creates a false sense of one's capabilities at a time when they could do better if they knew they had to. In the end, when it comes to getting a quality job it will be one's ability to perform that will determine success, not the "grade" in school. If the grade was misleading, it is the student who will suffer first. If enough students across the nation are misled, it is our country that will suffer.

Here is a case in point. I talked to a recruiter for a large information services company about the quality of people she was interviewing. She told me that she was rejecting seven out of ten of the candidates she interviewed from local colleges and universities. Specifically, she cited poor communication skills, the inability to read and understand what was written, the inability to write a cohesive thought, the inability to present ideas clearly to a group. These skills, she contends, are ones that should have been *developed in junior high school* and *honed in high school*. They are not the skills that a corporation should have to teach remedially in the workplace. Yet the grades of all the applicants were high enough to indicate that they should have been proficient in each of these skills.

The real test of an applicant comes when he or she comes face to face with corporate recruiters or begins a job. It is at this point that the quality of the individual is demonstrated. All of one's education, poise and character are exposed, tested, assessed and rated. Grades on paper only get you to the interview or to the job. The real grades come after.

Warning: The essential job skills can be learned and applied globally—and they are. The result will be that, if a segment of the world cannot produce people with the skills needed for success, corporations must, and will, relocate the jobs to where they can find the human resources. It may not be in your son's or daughter's back yard.

We owe it to our sons and daughters to talk openly and directly about the challenges that they will face and about the real condition of our country's strengths. Only with complete and accurate knowledge will we be able to build a really competitive advantage.

We owe it to our sons and daughters to support and encourage them, to help them find their way toward their future, and to work with them to build on their strengths and their loves, for that is where they will be happiest and most productive.

We owe it to our sons and daughters to let them know that grades are a reflection of their performance in a given skill or discipline, not on them as people. Low grades on a test or in a course don't mean they are without value, just like high grades don't guarantee future success in life. However, grades *are* signals. They can indicate that no effort was put forth to study. They can highlight poor study habits or problems with peers. As a parent, we also owe it to our kids to get to the underlying causes for low grades and take the steps to resolve them.

Action Steps

If we were together, I would emphasize

* Your teen's life will be filled with challenges that are unlike those that you faced. It is up to you to show your teen what that future is going to look like. It is up to you to tell him or her what will be needed to succeed. It is up to you to provide the best support and guidance you can. *It is up to your teen to do his or her best to prepare for the journey. It is your teen's responsibility to create his or her path.*

1. William J. Bennett, The Index mof Leading Cultural Indicators, New York: Simon & Schuster, p.83
2. ibid., p.86

2— Job Opportunities

In the appendix you will be exposed to a wide variety of job opportunities that are unfolding in two to eight years as projected by the Bureau of Labor Statistics. The agency lists over 250 separate categories of occupations, from executives to waiters and waitresses. I've provided descriptions for the categories with the largest numbers of job openings and the fastest growing industries. In addition, there is a chart that reports the earnings of recent college graduates by sex and by major field of study.

It is estimated that over half the jobs that will become available in your teen's working lifetime have yet to be created. This makes sense when you consider the number of changes occurring right now and the pace of those changes. Jobs like web page designers and video game software developers were unheard of just a few years ago. More and more, as new areas of endeavor (from communication to biotechnology to space travel), open up or expand, they will require enhanced or totally new skills, new languages and new ways of thinking.

At this stage of his or her life, your teen should look at all the types of work that interest him or her. In fact, it makes good sense to take the broad view. But, don't just make a list of job names. Ask your teen to imagine for thirty seconds that he or she *is* the person doing that job. Ask him or her to try to get the sense and feel of it. Is it comfortable? How does he or she feel doing it? What is he or she experiencing? What are the skills needed to do the job well? Does he or she have them? At their leisure, they should go on to another job and try it on.

For best results, ask your teen to make a record of his or her thoughts and feelings about each job and of the skills that have been identified. Then compare the list he or she has made to a published list of requirements for the job, which you can get from the high school career counselor, the local library or the Bureau of Labor Statistics.

If you've considered a number of jobs, look for similarities in the skills required. Your teen will be amazed at how many skills are *common* to numerous unrelated fields. For example, interpersonal skills (the ability to get along with and influence others), communication skills (the ability to organize thoughts, express them, and have others understand them) are essential skills that apply to almost all human interaction. They are as applicable in an engineering office as they are at an accounting firm or the NASA space agency. Ask your teen, " Knowing what you know now, how will you approach the courses you are taking in school?"

Let's start with the sciences:

Medicine

Within this field lies the need for *researchers* to uncover cures for diseases that afflict great numbers of people - from Alzheimer's, which slowly attacks a person's mind until he or she no longer has a memory, to AIDS, which is decimating societies, especially in Asia and Africa. Imagine that your son or daughter is a part of the team that solves one major mystery. How would you feel knowing that his or her contribution would impact millions of people all over the world? There are *plastic surgeons* who leave their practices once a year and spend time in out-of-the way villages in impoverished countries and use their talents to reconstruct the scarred faces of children. Imagine that your son or daughter is the doctor who repaired a child's cleft lip and freed her to live a normal life, free from ridicule. Think of the burden your child would lift from both the patient and her parents. Try to feel the gratitude they would express. How would you feel about your son or daughter giving those gifts?

Demand is even greater for registered nurses, medical assistants, home health aides and nursing aides. This group will account for 1.6 million new jobs out of the expected 2.7 million new jobs for health occupations as a whole. The aging of America will offer great jobs for the life of your career. There are others, from pediatricians to heart and lung specialists to neurosurgeons. Think about them, research their work, ask yourself, "What if my son or daughter...?"

Engineering

We are exposed to the work of engineers in

every facet of our lives. Design engineers were instrumental in bringing us innovations in everything from cars to refrigerators to furniture and the fasteners that hold them together. We would not be flying, driving or even riding bicycles but for the ideas of engineers. Engineers gave us the memory in computer hard-disk drives, durable automobiles and washing machines, the circuit boards that fill everything from cars to televisions. The Olympic Village in Atlanta was constructed of composite materials with the strength of steel and the lightness of plastic. The entire village was designed to be collapsed onto truck beds (which were part of the construction) and sent elsewhere for reuse — including all the utilities! Much of the technology used in this project was a result of knowledge gained from the space programs.

Don't overlook the new engineering fields such as ceramics, genetic engineering, biotechnology or telecommunications. Could your teen be an engineer? The second fastest growing cluster of new jobs, engineers, natural scientists, mathematicians, system analysts and computer scientists will add over 1.3 million jobs through 2005.

Education

Why would your son or daughter want to be a teacher? Perhaps because of a strong need to give of him or herself and to share knowledge with others; to develop minds and mold ideas. Your teen could mentor students to find the lives that are most rewarding for them. If he or she could be visited years from now by appreciative former students who have come back to say "thanks" for all they've received, would that be something he or she would find fulfilling?

Education - related occupations will add some 2 million jobs by 2005, both in public and private services. The jobs will vary from secondary school and special education teachers to teachers aides and counselors.

Food, Cleaning, Personal and Protective Services

Growth in the first three categories (Food, Cleaning, and Personal Services) will be faster than the average because increasing numbers of people are working. They will be eating out more. They will have less time to take care of personal chores, like housekeeping, so they will hire other people to do them.

Growth in the travel and tourism industry is creating demands for chefs, with salaries often above $80,000 per year at upscale resorts.

Growing concerns about safety will increase the demand for protection, from guards at apartment complexes to increased security at shopping centers. With the growth of prisons comes work for prison guards, with salaries in excess of $25,000 per year, plus benefits.

While the number of jobs projected is significant (over half a million), the jobs are, for the most part, low paying and have high turnover rates.

The jobs that aren't - yet.

There are literally thousands of job classifications listed by the U.S. Government Department of Labor. In your teen's lifetime you might have jobs that don't exist today. These jobs will be necessary, challenging and rewarding. Some will occur in aerospace as the country moves toward its first attempts to station people in space. Others will result from evolutionary growth and expansion in communication technologies. Still more will come in advances in medicine and biotechnology.

Will your son or daughter be ready? If he or she prepares now, and remains adaptable, the answer can be yes.

Preparation comes through learning the essentials — reading, writing, math and sciences — and supplementing them with advanced learning in critical thinking skills, problem identification and problem solving skills and systems thinking.

The key to learning these skills is balance. Your teen doesn't have to do it all at once. Nor does he or she have to do it all. As a high school student, your teen has time to assess his or her future: to plan and lay out his or her objectives, to investigate and experiment, and to modify and change. Getting a solid footing in the basics gives him or her a solid foundation on which to build just about anything.

Caution: As your teen thinks about the things he or she might like to do, understand that until he or she *tries* them, they'll only be a "thought" or a gut feeling that has not been put to the test.

Here's an example. I had a friend who always dreamed of being a nurse - until the summer she volunteered as a candy striper at the local hospital. She hated it! She didn't like the noise, the frantic pace, the smells or administering aid. She was glad she found it out early and before she committed to a career.

Action Steps

If we were together, I would emphasize

* Encourage your teen to be daring and test his or her instincts. If he or she finds that she has missed the mark, she is, in fact, ahead of the game. She eliminated one possibility and can now move ahead to test another.
* This is the time in your teen's life to try many things. Encourage him or her to use the time well.

Action Steps

* There are many things we'd like to do because, on the surface, we see them as noble or exciting or interesting. Tell your teen not to base her judgments on superficial feelings. Test the concepts before continuing.

3— The Changing Structure of Work

Now let's take a look at work from another perspective, classifying work into only three large categories: production work, in-person work, and knowledge work. In large part, this comes from the writings of Robert B. Reich, Secretary of Labor in the Clinton Administration, a member of Harvard University's John F. Kennedy School of Government, and a leading political economist.

There are major differences between the three categories and also within them: the kind of work done in each group, where the work can be done, salaries that can be expected, and the futures of each category. I urge you to read this chapter closely for it is one of the most important in the book, along with the chapter on skills. Better still, read Reich's book. It's exceptional.

Production work is work that is done repetitively, in high volumes, requiring relatively low skill. These jobs include work like assembling cars, sewing clothes, or flipping hamburgers at a fast food restaurant. They also include data entry, like typing a manuscript, billing customers, or inputting data into insurance forms. Workers in this category don't come into contact with the end users. Their work environment is an open layout with hundreds of people doing the same types of work. Their performance is judged by their output, which is measured in units: so many wheels or shirts or invoices per hour, day, or week. Employers want people who can follow the rules, are reliable and loyal. Educational requirements in the U.S. call for a high school diploma or equivalent. In most other countries, there are no such requirements.

Pay can vary dramatically, depending on where the job is located and the presence or absence of a strong union. An auto assembly worker in the U.S. makes a much better wage than the assembly employee in a non-union U.S. shop. An auto assembly worker at Chrysler in China earns $3,600 per year; his counterpart in the U.S. can earn ten times that or more. A Brazilian shoe factory worker earns only about $56 per month!

Taken as a whole, production workers are mostly non-white and female. Production work accounts for about 25 percent of all workers, but it is declining due to outsourcing and automation.

In-person work is done wherever the customers who benefit from it are. In-person jobs include such diverse occupations as plumber, carpenter, physical therapist, taxi driver, bar tender, and hotel housekeeper. Most workers in this category come into contact with the end-user. These people usually work alone or in small groups. Employers look for people who, like production workers, are reliable, loyal, and can take orders. Since most of these employees come into contact with their clients or the company's clients, they must also be pleasant and personable.

Earnings vary widely in this group as well. Housekeepers and waitresses earn much less than physical therapists, dental hygienists, or translators.

Education levels also vary, from high school or equivalent to specialized vocational training to a four year college degree. The majority of workers in this classification—which accounts for almost a third of the labor force—are women. As you'll recall from the job projections, this category will grow very fast in the next decade.

Knowledge workers, called *symbolic analysts* by Reich, operate in just about all industries, using skills in problem identification and problem solving, conceptual thinking and communication to provide their services across the globe. This category includes scientists and engineers, computer software developers, lawyers, real estate developers, marketing and sales professionals, writers, film producers, and musicians to name just a few.

[margin note: This is what I do, for instance.]

Knowledge workers can work alone or in small groups. They can form temporary alliances to do a single job, or they may form long-lasting associations. Knowledge workers spend most of their time on identifying opportunities (problems), and coming up with the answers (solutions). Think of movie producers, writers and actors who collaborate on a movie and, once the movie is completed, move on to other associations. There are no lifetime contracts here. Each person is involved because his or her skills and talents "fit" the need of the moment.

If you own a computer modem, you know that inside the box it came in were the modem itself and the software to run it. Each was made by a different company. Each company warranties only its own component. Each mails out announcements regarding its own upgrades. Imagine how important team work is to the end result. If one company's contribution doesn't perform to standards, that company might disappear from existence.

Most knowledge workers are white males. Non-whites and women are increasing in numbers and influence. Earnings vary according to the nature of the job and service provided, from tens of thousands of dollars to millions. Earnings are the best of the three categories. It is from this group that the best life styles come.

Currently, about 20 percent of the available jobs are in this group. Growth in this area is limited and competition will become even more intense as increasing numbers of people around the world gain the knowledge and skills to participate. Just as production work has been able to go off-shore, so has knowledge work. Even so, this is where the best opportunities lie.

Making a Choice

When you think about your teen's place in the future, encourage him or her to try to achieve a balance between the things he or she loves to do and the quality of life he or she wants to have. Often, with planning, a person can have a great life doing something that he or she loves to do. If your teen would like that, too, then have him or her try this exercise:

* Draw three large circles on paper. In the first circle list all the things you love to do, regardless of how good you are at doing them. In the second, list all the things you do really well, regardless of whether you like to do them. From these two circles, select all the things you love to do and are good to great at for the final circle. You'll probably have plenty of things in the third circle to consider as options for your future work. Many of

> The road to happiness lies in two simple principles: find what it is that interests you and that you can do well, and when you find it put your whole soul into it-- every bit of energy and ambition and natural ability you have.
>
> John D. Rockefeller III

> Life is to be lived. If you have to support yourself, you had bloody well better find some way that is going to be interesting. And you don't do that by sitting around wondering about yourself.
>
> Katharine Hepburn

> Starting out to make money is the greatest mistake in life. Do what you feel you have a flair for doing, and if you are good enough at it, the money will come.
>
> Greer Garson

them could provide you a financially comfortable living.

When you think about the different possibilities, look both at your passion for each possibility and the quality of life it would provide you if you pursued it full time. If the anticipated earnings for a career you'd love to pursue are satisfactory to you, put a check next to it and go on to evaluate another. You will have many more than one. If the career you find most desirable won't sustain the life style you need, you've got a decision to make. One option is to consider a different job that you find challenging and personally rewarding that can satisfy your financial needs as well. Then you can pursue your primary passion as an avocation or hobby.

There are many starving artists striving for their day of recognition. Your teen may elect to be one of them, saying, in effect, "forget the conventional life. I'm going to do what I need to do, indeed what I feel I must do. I'm willing to do whatever it takes to fulfill my dream. I'm willing to forego comforts if necessary." If that is your teen's choice, just be sure that he or she has thought it through. That being said, encourage your son or daughter to go for it. Not everyone starves.

An example is René, a graphic designer of good repute. She works with a number of large advertising agencies and marketing companies as well as a number of smaller companies that can't afford to use ad agencies. Her strengths lie in her natural ability to understand what clients need and to work with them to achieve it, whether its a large campaign or a simple brochure. She works with other independents who write the text or print the brochures.

In a similar fashion, my friend, Leonard, is an expert at locating new and used medical equipment. His reputation is global. People call on him to find equipment for them. Leonard is an independent problem solver—very good and very handsomely rewarded for his knowledge.

Both René and Leonard value their independence. René really likes working with a number of different colleagues on a variety of challenges. Leonard values money, lots of it. It buys him freedom. As the money comes in, he invests it in condos or stocks or whatever he thinks will be the best use of the money at the moment. Both see their best investment is in themselves.

Action Steps **If we were together, I would emphasize**

* Ask your teen to look closely at the areas that hold his or her most passionate interests. Look seriously at the economic prospects they offer. If they cannot sustain one person, let alone two or a family, ask your teen whether he or she can afford them in his or her life. Poverty *is* everything it's cracked up to be.

* Encourage your teen to consider other work that is both interesting and that can sustain the life style he or she wants. If a person makes a conscious decision to do something he or she loves, knowing that there is little financial future in it, so be it. The important thing is that he or she knows and accepts the risks.

• Life is, after all, finite. Living our mission is a dream we all have. Not all of us are blessed to live it.

4 — Skills Your Teen Will Need

Five sets of skills have been identified as essential for your teen's success in life. What is written here for you is different than what is in the Teen's book, so you might want to read both sections. In this section I have been direct in a different fashion to help you when you are talking with your son or daughter. Writing and oral communications are separated out to give each the special attention it deserves.

It will take a lot of work on your teen's part to master the skills outlined. The tough part is mustering the will and sustaining the attitude to carry on. Your support and encouragement will improve his or her chances of success tremendously. Help your teen create a vision of the exciting outcomes that await him or her at the end of the journey: the moment of graduation with honors, the acceptance to a first rate college, recognition from family and friends on a job well done. Create any and all of these pictures in his or her mind as outcomes that he or she wants and can achieve. Infuse the vision with *passion*, one of the greatest energizers we know. Need a reason? Make a

[Margin note: Specific, Measurable, Achievable, Realizable, Time-based]

reason! Make it clear, achievable, and realistic, and wrap it in a time frame. Don't let anyone put it off. (Use the acronym SMART to help you create goals. In order for goals to be effective, they must be Specific, Measurable, Achievable, Realizable and Time-based).

Communication skills

This cluster of skills is the most important to recruiters with whom I have spoken personally. The answers to the first few questions in an interview tell the recruiter many things about the applicant. They show how he or she has prepared for the interview, how he or she listens, organizes his or her thoughts, thinks under pressure, manages time, and undertakes an assignment.

A person's writing does the same thing. It clarifies for the reader how the author approached the topic, how he or she organized the research and structured the final document. The choice of vocabulary reflects the author's command of the language and the depth of his or her thinking.

Large companies are having such a serious

problem finding people who can communicate that they've had to contract with training organizations to educate their employees. Think of the advantage that proficiency in this area can give to your teen. Think of the disadvantage he or she faces without it.

If your sons or daughters cannot communicate clearly when speaking or writing, get them working now to change the situation. Talk to your teen about testing his or her skills in this area and getting remedial help while he or she is still in high school. If it is necessary to get help from outside the school, do it. Now is the time to invest in your teen. Now is the time to show them that all the work they'll have to do is an investment in themselves.

Second Languages

A friend recently asked me the following questions: "What do you call a person who speaks two languages?"
"Bilingual," I replied.
"Right, so what do you call a person who speaks more than two languages?"
"Multilingual."
"Great! Now what do you call a person who

> The real secret of success is enthusiasm. Yes, more than enthusiasm, I would say excitement. I like to see men get excited. When they get excited they make a success of their lives.
> Walter Chrysler

> The passions are the only orators which always persuade.
> Francois de La Rochefoucauld

speaks *one* language?"

"Monolingual?," I asked, somewhat puzzled.

"<u>American</u>!" he said, laughing out loud. (Share this with your teen.)

The world has grown smaller, and many of the people in it who have improved their education are reaping the benefits of their labors. Interestingly, while people from around the globe have studied us, learned our language, and assessed the good and bad of our culture, we have done little to internalize their languages or to improve our understanding of their cultures. As a result, we are at a competitive disadvantage with other nations.

The bulk of the people in this hemisphere speak Spanish or Portuguese. They, for decades, were considered third world. Yet today, Chile has a stronger economy than ours by many criteria. Brazil and Argentina are the fastest growing nations in this hemisphere. Mexico, in spite of its many problems, has within its borders numerous foreign manufacturing facilities employing thousands of Mexican graduate engineers.

> The population of Japan accounts for about 2.5% of the world's total population, yet look at the influence this nation has had on our globe. Imagine the impact you can have when you master the language and learn the culture.

The output of some Japanese transplant companies in Mexico is better than the output from the plants in Japan. Many of these workers speak Japanese and English as well as Spanish. This gives them a definite competitive advantage in the new global economy.

Learning a second language is more than conjugating verbs or building a vocabulary. Learning a second language is learning a second culture, with all the subtleties that implies. It means internalizing the ways in which people communicate, the ways they structure their thinking, and developing an empathy with them. It means growing closer. It means personal growth. It can also mean a great job opportunity. A friend of my son, who is fluent in Japanese, was hired upon graduation from college by one of the big three auto companies for that skill. His salary is over $50,000 per year! How's that for an incentive? A public speaker I know was told that if he could deliver his talk in Spanish and answer audience questions in Spanish, he could earn $10,000 an hour!

Ni hui bu hui shuo Zhong Guo hua? If you are fluent in Chinese, you can speak to 20% of the world's population.

Encourage your son or daughter to apply serious effort in gaining command of a second language and culture. If you can manage it, send him or her to a foreign country for a few weeks or months to gain insights into the cultures first-hand. You'll give the gift of a lifetime.

In the small Mexican city of Guanajuato, a university town, there is a school called Instituto Falcón. People from all over the world go there to learn Spanish. Courses from basic to advanced Spanish are supplemented with classes on Mexican history and many others. The price for a week's immersion in this delightful language is $150. Surely other similar schools exist around the world. This is a fun way to learn, to make global friendships and to enhance one's life experiences.

Time Management and Study Skills

Time management

> Live mindful of how brief your life is.
>
> Horace

The single greatest stressor on people comes from not having enough time, yet most people don't use time to their advantage; hence, they lose it. Entire industries have been built on teaching people how to organize and manage their time. Perhaps the best question your teen (or you) will ever ask is "Is this the best use of my time right now?"

You know first-hand all the pressures on your time. As a parent, you are the bread winner or the homemaker (or both). You serve many masters: your boss, the family, your aging parents, and the organizations in which you volunteer. You shop, taxi the kids, cook, listen, and give emotional support and love. It may all seem like a blur at times.

It's often that way for your teens. They have social obligations, jobs of their own, school, and studies to maintain. They have to make sure to get to band practice or the playing field, to work, or to the library. They rely on you or their friends for support.

Imagine how much better life could be, if only you could get it all together. Imagine how much easier things could be if everyone accepted responsibility for themselves, planned ahead, and communicated their needs.

> Lost time is never found again.
>
> Benjamin Franklin

> Minutes are worth more than money. Spend them wisely.
>
> Thomas P. Murphy

> To do two things at once is to do neither.
>
> Pubilius Syrus

That's what this section is all about.

Study skills

The value of good study habits increases in high school and college. During any given college semester, a student will be expected to read or research from dozens of books and articles. Disciplined study habits will help your student do this successfully.

Study habits are more than making good use of time. Mastering good study habits develops personal discipline, focus, and critical thinking skills. Good study habits include techniques that help a student identify and then focus on learning what's important. A good book on study habits teaches the student how to read course materials to get the essentials without reading each word. It teaches that the essence of a book can be gleaned by reading the summary first, followed by the first sentences of each paragraph. A good book on study habits will also give great tips on how to write papers and how to prepare to take tests. Using the lessons of such books can cut study time and produce better results as well.

> Successful minds work like a gimlet: to a point.
>
> Christian Bovee

There are any number of good books and tapes on studying, time management, and organization skills. A list of some of them is included in the appendix.

Socialization Skills

Each skill included in this cluster is individually essential. Combined, they are even more powerful.

Listening skills —top the list of social skills because they are perhaps the most powerful skills one can develop. Everyone wants to be heard, but few want to listen. People who refine listening skills develop deep, meaningful relationships with others. By demonstrating the ability to understand another's point of view, they build a bond that is meaningful and valued.

A good listener facilitates team building, resolves conflicts easily, and is sought out in social circles. A good listener is usually also a good student because he or she understands the subjects taught with greater depth. A good listener has greater self-awareness because he or she hears the inner voice as well as external

No man ever became wise by chance.

Lucius Annaeus Seneca

conversations.

Conflict resolution — is a necessary skill in any organization. Even people who share the same mission will often differ on how to achieve it. Given the broad range of personality types in any organization and the number of ways people can devise to achieve goals, conflict of some sort is inevitable—and desirable. Healthy conflict helps clarify ideas and opportunities, tests various alternatives, and brings people together. Good conflict-resolution skills are the mark of both a leader and a supporter. Conflict resolvers gain consensus and achieve outcomes that are appreciated by all parties.

Team building — and collaboration are a result of the growing understanding of just how much we need one another. Rugged individuality has given way to cooperation.

Your teen will gain a big benefit from learning team building. A team relies on all its members for success. If some members are not contributing, the group learns how to deal with them. They either convince them of the goals

> Happiness is not the absence of conflict, but the ability to cope with it.
>
> Unknown

or they throw them off the team. This can be a strong lesson for your teen when he or she is selecting her friends. If your teen wants to accomplish things in her lifetime, but the peers she hangs out with don't share the same vision, it is time for her to make some hard decisions. It's impossible to hang around with nay sayers or slackers without being caught up with the negativity. If your teen wants to achieve, she'll have to make a conscious choice of social contacts. That's a powerful lesson to learn.

> Keep away from people who try to belittle your ambitions. Small people always do that, but the really great make you feel that you, too, can become great.
>
> Mark Twain

Achievers are a wonderful lot. They support one another emotionally, spiritually and intellectually. I marvel as I think of the many ways my sons grew in their associations. Chris with the Boy Scouts, the high school marching band and in martial arts; Aaron, in the theater group, in his fraternity and as a student council member in college. The growth through these associations helped round each boy out as it helped him academically. I wish your son or daughter similar good fortune.

Manners are becoming increasingly rare at a time when the need for them is growing in importance. You can call them simple manners, from how to say hello, to making an introduction; from table manners to phone courtesies.

The best way to learn and refine social skills is through training. Many small companies market programs for social skills development. If you feel that your teen's skills could use improvement, make the investment to teach them. The effort will be worth it in the long run.

Interviewing skills — is a combination of many skills, including thinking, planning and socialization.

Many people think of interviewing as one sided, wherein one person asks all the questions and the other attempts to answer them with the intent of making a good impression and getting a job.

A good interview is actually an exercise in which both people try to get to know one another. Their mutual objective is to find out what they have in common and where they might differ, to see if there is a fit. In addition to sharing questions and answers, people also note each others manners and personal behaviors. To many, a person's behavior style is as important as his knowledge or skills. Think back to the old expression, "You can dress him up, but you can't take him out."

Here is an example. A person was on an interview that went longer than expected, so his host invited him to lunch at a posh restaurant. Everything was going well until, at the end of the lunch, the prospect asked the waiter for a doggie bag for his leftovers. That one gesture cost him the job.

In preparing for an interview a person needs to look inside and ask questions like, "What kind of work excites me?" "What kind of environment do I want to work in?" "What skills do I bring to an employer?" "What are my attitudes?" This is not important just because the employer may ask exactly those questions. It is also important so a person can assess whether the prospective employer is a fit for him or her.

You now know what millions of people don't—that the interview is as much for you as it is for an employer. By knowing what is important to you, you can weed out employment opportunities that don't fit you!

Share that with your teen. Prepare a list of the questions an interviewer would ask. Then ask your teen to write down his or her personal answers to each question as an exercise in introspection and self-discovery. Try it yourself. You'll be amazed at what you learn.

Systems Thinking

The world has grown so much more complex since we were students. In addition to the problems highlighted earlier, our children will face many other issues as adult members of their communities. They include increasing numbers of prisons, an aging population (us), global warming, pollution from hazardous wastes, political instability, and numerous others. All of these problems are complex. There are no easy solutions. It is critical that our teens receive training in problem solving and systems thinking to deal with them.

Systems thinking is looking at how things work together over time. It's big picture thinking. You try to look for patterns of behavior that explain how and why things are the way they are. In systems thinking, you realize that you are a part of the system, not a bystander. Your actions can have an affect on the system you're in. That affect can be positive, negative or neutral.

Here are a couple examples of systems thinking:

- Some forty years ago, a handful of politicians passed some laws reducing tariffs and duties on shoes produced in South America. At the time, the only people who were concerned about these moves were executives from U.S. shoe companies who saw it as a threat. They talked to their congressmen, who told them not to worry. Today, there are only a couple shoe manufacturers left in the U.S. Thousands of American jobs were lost over time.

- On a blistering hot day in Los Angeles, two men, strangers to one another, start to fight on the Santa Ana Freeway. Both were stressed out and tired of the hour-long traffic jam all around them. One looked at the other and that look sparked a chain of verbal exchanges and hand gestures that led to the fight.

This is not a random act as much as it is a *system* failure. The traffic jam keeps everyone locked up. Individual stresses mount. Each person is thinking of the impact of the delays on himself or herself. We all handle stressors differently. This is a systems problem that people must address with the goal of making things better.

Training in systems thinking gives people the tools they need to understand how things work, how they can work better, and how they can deal with changes productively.

Computers and the Internet

The communications revolution has, for all intents and purposes, brought everyone together in real time. There is very little that we can do in the United States that cannot be done as well or better at other points on the globe—and cheaper. What will separate us are the quality of our minds and our abilities to produce. That edge is fragile. The same holds true for everyone else on the globe.

Changes in telecommunications are happening so fast that we have a hard time keeping up with them. Books written about telecommunication topics are obsolete before they reach the stores. Millions of people will learn about the changes in the world wide web by being on the internet itself through their personal computer. Millions of students will learn the latest about subjects they are researching *faster* than their professors—and that poses a serious problem for teachers.

Think of teaching and learning as a pyramid. At the top is the professor, steeped in knowledge. He has spent years learning and has become the source of specialized knowledge. At the base are his students who have come in search of that knowledge and enlightenment.

Today, however, students can access all the professor's knowledge *and* all of the latest advances in his field from the world wide web. In fact, students who are capable "web surfers" actually get ahead of their professors because often the old guard is reluctant to adapt to and use new technologies like the web. In effect, where once they were experts, professors can become dinosaurs. The web will be the great equalizer.

Currently, the U.S. has the blessing of having more computers per capita than any other country. This advantage will not remain with us long. Your teen should get up to speed on the significance of global communications and the opportunities it affords to prepared students.

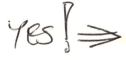

It is essential that teens get on the world wide web and uses it for all the good it has to offer. It is the greatest research source ever. They can produce excellent reports for class using the web. It is also a way to meet really great people across the globe. You and your teens can use the web as a way to start a business from home or as a way to find exciting job opportunities. The web is to us today what the automobile was to our great grandparents—a liberator.

Financial Planning Skills

Financial planning skills are normally learned as one goes along. It makes learning more meaningful to use real money. Today, it is important that teens learn this skill early. Two reasons are time and the leveling of incomes. As you and I planned out our lives, we assumed that we would work at one place until retirement at 65. Today, millions of people are receiving their severance at 55 or younger. The years during which many of us planned to earn the highest salaries and have decreasing expenses are disappearing rapidly.

> Share this with your teenager: Invest $100 each month for 45 years at 10% compound interest and you'll have over $850,000 for your retirement

Looking ahead, the picture is less inviting for our children. The median income will drop by some 20 percent over the next decade for many. Even the wages for knowledge workers will be limited by global competition. Therefore, your children should learn money management skills and apply them earlier. They will have to manage their earnings with greater caution than we did.

Many college students learn about financial planning the hard way — by amassing credit card debt. Credit card companies deluge campuses with their applications. They buy mailing lists of students from colleges and send their applications directly.

For many students, the desire to get their first credit card is overwhelming. It is proof of their independence. Unfortunately, using the card is far easier than paying the bill. The excitement of the moment often overrules common sense.

Parents often find themselves in a quandary. When their students calls home, thousands of dollars in debt, they are often not sure if they should bail them out or let them learn a painful lesson. Some parents have no choice. Teaching solid financial self-defense early will reduce the threat of financial ruin.

There are any number of good books on financial management. Many great shows about financial planning air on National Public Television. One, *The Wealthy Barber*, is both easy to understand and fun to watch. The point I leave you with is that your teen must take responsibility early on for this important aspect of his or her personal life.

Stress Management

We have all experienced stress, some more severe than others. The stress associated with the changing nature of work will increase over the next decade and beyond as the economy unavoidably changes. The stress levels on students and families will increase as the ability of many to cope with the new realities wanes.

One way to look at stress is to define it as a conflict between reality and our perceptions of reality. When there is a mismatch, there is conflict. Looked at in this context, it's not hard to see why stress levels are so high. Yet it is also not hard to see how to relieve some of the stress — by adjusting our perceptions.

For example, imagine that one person is concerned that there are so many different ethnic groups with their own languages that English should be made the national language. He finds this stressful. It represents a major change that he doesn't like, yet feels helpless to do anything about it. Another person, seeing the same change, applies himself to use the language skills he first learned in high school and refined in college. He finds himself at home with the people of this ethnic group. He finds himself deeply respected by the members of this group because he took the time to learn their language and to appreciate their rich culture. He is influential.

Stress can be minimized in other ways as well: through meditation, yoga, martial arts like tai chi, through exercise and hobbies, through medicine and support groups, and through therapy, both psychological and physical. A great massage can work wonders on the spirit. If you feel the need for stress relief, recognize that you are not alone. Find the help you need and take it.

Action Steps

If we were together, I would emphasize

- Many of these skills can be learned and honed in high school. Help your teen take advantage of this opportunity.

- Now is the time to invest. Seek out training for additional skills. Consider sending your teen to evening or week-end seminars during the school year or week-day seminars in the summer. **Action Steps**

- Stress will grow in intensity as the structural changes in the workplace take hold. Planning and solid follow-through will reduce the stress.

- Encourage your teen to learn stress management techniques. <u>Learn them yourself.</u>

5— Competition Your Teen Will Face

An estimated 39 million jobs will have opened up between 1994 and 2005. Roughly 23 million will be as replacements for people leaving the work force. Some 16 million new jobs will be added. In the Teenagers' Guide, we listed and described some of the major clusters and cited growth estimates as found in the *Occupational Outlook Quarterly* from the U.S. Department of Labor, Bureau of Labor Statistics (BLS). They include:

Job Category	Estimated # of New Jobs 1994-2005 (in millions)
Medicine	2.7
Education	2.0
Engineering	1.3
Total	6.0

These clusters represent only about 38 percent of the 16 million new jobs projected by the BLS. Nine million of the jobs projected are in lower-paying, service-sector jobs (food service, janitorial, waiting tables, cashiers, and sales clerks). Just under 1 million jobs are forecast in executive and general management, or systems analysts jobs, which command significantly better salaries. The bulk of the jobs will pay low to moderate salaries that barely sustain the wage earner alone. Within the broad categories listed in the chart are many low-paying jobs, such as health aides, teachers aides and educational assistants.

While the job clusters we're talking about are for domestic employment, you should be aware of the influence that world-wide employment will have on our country. Job growth will be slow (about 1 percent) *globally* over the next decade. With such slow progress in job creation, the competition for the best jobs will be intense everywhere. Therefore, it is increasingly important that your teen develop the skills he or she will need to compete for them.

Globalization is also quickly changing the economic structure of the world. One result will be the redistribution of incomes, as work that can be performed anywhere *will* be.

Here's an example that ties in with the section

on second languages. My friend, Richard, needed some promotional literature translated into Spanish. He had seen some competitive literature that had been poorly translated from English, and he knew the Mexican customers were ridiculing it. He also knew who the competition used to do the translation, and he found out that the cost to translate was 20 cents a word. He sent his promotional package to an interpreter in Guadalajara, Mexico, a woman proficient in English as well as Spanish. She delivered an excellent, top-quality product that was very well received by his Mexican customers. Richard's customers commented that they felt his company understood them better than his competition. They said this was demonstrated by the quality of the literature. Richard got better results, and paid only 20 pesos *(six cents)* per word.

Increasingly, competition based on price will result in a leveling of what can be charged anywhere in the world. The skills your teen will need are also being learned by educated people all over the globe. Soon it will be possible to price almost any service anywhere in the world and expect that the quality will be high. Global competition is pitting people who possess good skills, talents and abilities, but who live in different geographic locations, against one another for the same prize — a good paying job.

What qualifies as good pay varies widely by country. For instance, an aerospace engineer in Connecticut can earn six to seven thousand dollars per month—a good living to be sure. His counterpart in Russia earns $200 per month—also a good living, given the economic conditions there. Software developers in California and France earn $7,000 and $3,000 per month respectively. Their counterpart in India earns $1400 per month, where a custom made suit retails for $20 and lunch for five or six at a trendy restaurant is $10.

Where the skills are equal, an employer will look at other things like the infrastructure of the country (roads, utilities), and the economic concessions that respective governments will offer as incentives for the company to locate a plant. If these requirements are met satisfactorily, then wages become an issue—

the lower the better. These are the realities we all face as we head into the next millennium.

Americans have experienced this form of global competition in industries that are labor intensive, like shoe or textile manufacturing, even high volume, high-tech products like memory disks or circuit boards. The result has been the loss of millions of U.S. jobs to other countries, where people will do the manual work for $30-$50 per *month* and engineers will work for $1,400 per month. As a result, entire industries, like textiles and shoes have been virtually erased from the American landscape, leaving displaced workers behind. Today, high-tech jobs—those that were supposed to stay in the U.S.—are going abroad, often at the flip of a switch.

Not every company wants to leave. They are quite happy being domestic companies with domestic employees. But, to stay viable, they must remain competitive. U.S. companies that want a domestic work force are facing a problem that no one thought would be a problem, an undereducated work force. Companies need highly trained, energetic, and committed workers to compete. If they can't find the people they need, they'll be forced to go elsewhere. This is a critical issue for companies and prospective employees—and a significant opportunity for prepared, educated teens.

This means that our teens will have to develop excellent skills in whatever discipline they choose in order to remain competitive with global competitors and to keep U.S. business and industry strong.

At the risk of repeating myself, let's be clear on this point: it isn't so important that your teen know exactly what he or she wants to be at this point. What *is* important is that when he or she does decide, that no one can keep him or her from doing it. That means a solid effort in self-development and personal growth.

As a parent, you can tell your teen the truth about competing in the global economy. Don't dwell on it in a negative way—this only serves to discourage. Instead, look at it as a challenge. Strong competition is a good thing. It forces us to think harder, to unleash our creative energies to get better. Properly educated and motivated, our kids can achieve a good standard of living for themselves anywhere in the world.

Another area of competition our teens will face comes from within. Competition in the future will come from students who are just now entering kindergarten and early elementary school. On the surface, this wouldn't seem like anything new, but consider this: to date, few schools have embraced technology in the classrooms and use it consistently as a tool for stimulating learning. Most teens, as a result, may have only limited exposure to computers or the internet.

Children now entering school will have such experiences. They will be more conversant and comfortable with technology and its advances than your teens will—and that will place them at a competitive advantage over current high schoolers. Because they will be exposed much earlier in life, they will learn from teachers using different training techniques and technology. They will develop different ways of thinking and communicating. The skills they will have mastered by the time they enter high school will be more advanced than the skills teens now entering college have.

One way to stay ahead is to stay abreast of change and constantly assimilate new learning. Life long learning is an essential fact, not a cliché.

If we were together, I would emphasize **Action Steps**

* Invest and reinvest constantly.

* Invest in your personal growth and development.

* Invest your earnings for personal financial growth.

* Invest in your relationships with close friends, family, and loved ones.

* Establish and cultivate strong associations in business.

* Cherish and protect your reputation.

* Learn, Learn, Learn.

6 — Personal Issues

College is not for everyone.

In fact, college never has been for everyone. About 63 percent of high school graduates go on to colleges or universities. Of these entrants, some 40 percent drop out within the first year. The reasons for this are many:

- Most are simply not prepared for the transition.
- The workload is so much greater than experienced in high school.
- Professors are impersonal. They don't seem to care about students the way that high school teachers do.
- There is no organization or direction as high school students are accustomed to. All responsibility for success seems to fall on the student.

In fact, all of this is true, except the caring. The degree of concern varies by college. Larger research colleges seem less concerned with freshmen—and for good reason. One lesson of history is survival of the fittest. If one is not meant to be in college, best to find it out sooner than later. College is for mature students and those who can survive until they mature.

Given the statistics, it is important that you look critically (though lovingly) at your son or daughter as he or she approaches the sophomore through senior phase of high school. If you are convinced that college is in his or her future, you'd do well to get him or her to some campuses to see what college is like. If the visits inspire your teen, then it should show up in his or her approach to high school. His or her emphasis should show a greater bias toward study to improve performance. If he or she is already a top performer, you can't expect much higher grades, but you may see subtle changes. For example, you may see that your teen is starting to think more seriously about which college will be the best match.

Selecting the right college is more than finding one that's close (or far), or inexpensive (see Why You Selected the College You Did in the appendix). A college must also fit your student's goals and self image. An impersonal campus with 10,000 students may be too much for your teen. He or she may be back home in a few months, feeling like a failure, when a smaller school, with a focus on individual attention might have helped him or her blossom. (Please choose a book or two to read from the selected reading list, the earlier on the better.)

You'll see statistics showing that a college graduate will earn hundreds of thousands of dollars more than a high school graduate during the course of his or her career. The time frame for this earnings gap is 40 years—the theoretical life cycle of a worker. With the changes in the structure of work, these numbers are now considered suspect. The gaps may be even greater.

Also suspect is the availability of jobs for college graduates. This has always been the case, because the demand for all workers varies with the times. Currently, graduates in disciplines like engineering, computer sciences, and physical therapy are in demand. Graduates in history, philosophy, and social work are having a difficult time finding jobs. Roughly 15 percent of all graduates are getting jobs outside of their chosen fields of study. It is estimated that by the turn of the century, 25 percent of college graduates will enter the work force without job prospects.

Today's realities are quite different from decades past, and they point to difficult times ahead. At only 1 percent per year through the year 2005, the global rate of increase in jobs is similar to that of the U.S. At the same time, more and more qualified employees are coming into work forces around the globe. With changes in technology making it easy to move work around, employees in many countries can just as easily do jobs in the categories of production work and knowledge work as our children can. So, it is more important than ever that your teen be a "qualified" college graduate, as opposed to a diploma bearing college graduate.

Given the slow growth in employment, it is also wise to look at the amount of debt you want to incur. Many students are leaving college with loan repayment obligations and no jobs. This does not mean that your teen can't get into a great school. What it may mean is that you'll look harder at finding scholarship money. A number of good books on selecting colleges and funding the college experience are listed in the bibliography.

Problems faced by colleges— opportunities for you

Colleges and Universities are businesses, too. They have to look at demographics just as hard as any commercial corporation, from the auto giants to personal computer manufacturers. Institutions of higher education have grown in number for the past few decades to meet the demands for education, but now they are facing the tough reality that the market is saturated. Market share is no longer just a concept taught to business students—it is a cry heard in campus recruiting offices around the country.

On the bright side, this makes your negotiating position for scholarships and financial aid much stronger than in years past. On the down side, you have to be more careful about the stability of the institutions you consider.

Another major concern around campus these days is the how relevant colleges will be in the future. Many newer technologies, like the web, are changing so fast that colleges can't learn them effectively enough to make relevant courses. For example, many students of the Internet at one college complained that they already knew more from being on the web at home than they were getting from the course. This lead them to question, quite properly, the value of any degree in this field. Things are just moving too fast to keep up.

With the slow pace of job creation, many students are seeking majors that are more relevant to the times, such as starting and running their own businesses. In response, some colleges and universities, like the University of Texas in Austin have created entrepreneurship programs for students who want to create their own futures. In these programs, students get hands-on experience in setting up new businesses. Professors work closely with their students to test out their ideas for new businesses. Some students actually start their businesses while attending school and use their classmates as advisors, providing them with valuable training in the process.

Tools and Thinking

Colleges are still important to us for the same reason they have always been—to produce critical thinkers. While skills like surfing the internet and mastering communication technology are essential, they are just tools, much like a calculator. While a calculator's usefulness increases with the complexity of the problem, it is the mind of man that determines what goes into it. The need to develop men and women of intellectual depth is still a critical mission. The need to train these people in the use of the latest tools is, also, but the former is still by far the more important.

Applicants for Masters programs are required by certain colleges to pass entrance exams as part of the selection process. For business majors, it's the GMAT (Graduate Management Admissions Test); for law students, it's the L-SAT (Law School Admissions Test), and so on. Interestingly, the applicants who score highest in the GMAT (for business) are those with bachelors degrees in *Philosophy!* The reason is that they can better understand the questions posed and have honed reasoning skills. It makes one wonder why liberal arts graduates don't fare better upon graduation.

The Case for Lifelong Learning

One lesson your son or daughter should learn as early as possible is that he or she will be expected to be a life long learner. People who continuously learn new ideas, and new methods of working and creating value have the best assurance of a long, productive, and economically sound working life. People who elect to "stay with what they know" will find themselves extinct—out of work or working at menial, low paying jobs.

It is essential that we all understand that continuous learning involves continuous reinvestment in learning. If a company provides for ongoing training, it should be considered a plus. The actual responsibility for determining what training is needed, and for getting it, is up to the individual.

As an example, let me share the story of a person we'll call Joe. Joe had worked for some fifteen years as a field salesman when his boss, a regional manager, announced his retirement. "Great," Joe thought. " Here's my chance to move up." He announced his desire to be considered for the job. Even though he was given the courtesy of an interview, it was clear that he wasn't going to get the job. He couldn't demonstrate that he had the necessary skills. Angrily, he confided to a friend and coworker that he felt it was his boss's fault for not giving him any training to prepare him to assume greater responsibilities. Because of his boss's neglect or deliberate inattention, he would miss out on the chance of his lifetime.

Joe's friend remained quiet for a few minutes after listening to him. When he did speak, he said, "You know, Joe, when I started with this company eight years ago, you had already been here for five. I had no degree. I was hired for my industry experience. In these eight years I made it my personal goal to get my bachelors degree. And I did. The company paid 80 percent of the costs. I also attended eight seminars on different facets of our business which the company paid for in full. Each time I achieved a goal, I also increased my value to my company. Each time I increased my personal worth because I can take this knowledge anywhere and use it to my advantage. What have you done in your thirteen years to increase your value?"

Joe was slow to respond. "I didn't do anything. But I would have if my boss had told me to, if he had shown me one bit of encouragement. Still, I do a great job selling every day. That's got to be worth something."

> What we prepare for is what we shall get.
>
> William Graham Sumner

"It is," the friend replied, "You are valued for the great job you do, and your skills are good enough for the job you are doing—but only for that job. Your lack of initiative has left you short of the skills needed for the next step. Joe, I think they made a wise move. I'm sorry."

Businesses need people with advanced skills. Many will support employees who demonstrate the desire to improve themselves.

Investing in yourself, even if you have to pay the bills personally, gives you skills that you can use anywhere. It gives you the option of deciding for yourself the company for which you will work.

It is essential that you teach your teen about the concept of value. As long as your teen knows who is responsible for his or her life and accepts that responsibility, he or she retains a valuable edge in the game of life.

Consider this from the noted and acclaimed historians, Will and Ariel Durant: "Nature smiles at the union of freedom and equality in our utopias. For freedom and equality are sworn and everlasting enemies, and when one prevails the other dies. Leave men free, and their natural inequalities will multiply almost geometrically, as in England and America in the nineteenth century under *laissez*-faire. To check the growth of inequality, liberty must be sacrificed, as in Russia after 1917. Even when repressed, inequality grows; only the man who is below the average in economic ability desires equality; those who are conscious of superior ability desire freedom; and in the end superior ability has its way.

Utopias of equality are biologically doomed, and the best that the amiable philosopher can hope for is an approximate equality of legal justice and educational opportunity. A society in which all potential abilities are allowed to develop and function will have a survival advantage in the competition of groups. This competition becomes more severe as the destruction of distance intensifies in confrontation of states." [1]

The Roles of Heroes

There is much talk about the need for heroes today. When we think of heroes, we think of people who are extraordinary, whether real or fictional. Some heroes are people of legend, from Hercules to the late President John F. Kennedy or Martin Luther King. To many, the late actor, John Wayne, was a hero, though he never fought a battle that wasn't on the screen.

Heroes can be just plain folk who rise to a situation when others are stymied. One example is a young teen who comes from the back of the school bus to take over the wheel when the driver has had a heart attack.

> The most important single influence in the life of a person is another person who is worthy of emulation.
>
> Paul D. Shafer

> Lives of great men all remind us we can make our lives sublime; and, departing, leave behind us, footprints on the sands of time.
>
> Henry Wadsworth Longfellow

Most people don't see themselves as heroic. Like this boy, they see themselves as doing what had to be done at the time. In that way, many are heroes. You may be a hero to your family, for the courage of convictions you espouse, for the discipline and vision you bring to their lives, for the way you live yours.

It is important that you talk to your teen about his or her heroes. This is a way of helping him or her assess the characteristics of heroes that are most important to him or her. It is a way of helping one clarify one's values, and to learn forgiveness as well.

No person, hero or not, is flawless. John F. Kennedy swam miles to shore from his destroyed PT boat (109), pulling a wounded comrade with him. He showed great courage during the Cuban missile crisis by preventing Russia from installing missiles that would threaten U.S. security from Cuban soil. The fact that he had affairs with numerous women shows that he was also flawed. One may call him a hero and forgive him the faults. Another may minimize his accomplishments, pointing only to his infidelities.

What traits are important to your teen? How will his or her idols influence the way he or she conducts his or her life and the choices made? Heroes serve to support us during our most difficult and trying times. We find ourselves asking, "How would our hero have handled this situation?" The answers then give us guidance and the strength to carry on, to succeed in the face of adversity. If a person is faced with a question of personal responsibility, he or she may ask, "How would JFK have responded?" Thinking back to the PT109 incident, he or she will remember that Jack had a choice. An accomplished swimmer, he could have easily elected to swim the great distance to shore alone—or he could accept responsibility for his shipmate and tow the man with him at great personal risk. Jack had a choice, and he made it. A lesson like this can help others during their times of decision.

The Roles of Teachers

Teachers historically served as instructors for our children. The best have assumed much larger roles, from mentors to spiritual leaders, encouraging their students to participate more,

> A teacher affects eternity; he can never tell where his influence stops.
>
> Henry (Brooks) Adams

to do more, and to be more. They brought enthusiasm, vigor, focus and love of the subject to countless numbers of eager learners. Neither you nor I had the full complement of such teachers. They simply don't exist in great numbers. Neither do perfect students.

Teaching has changed out of necessity, as evidenced by the chart at the beginning of the book. Teachers simply have many more things to do *in addition to teaching.* They are baby sitters, wardens, administrators, and pseudo parents for many children who don't have their own. All this for less money than they would get working on the production line at one of the big three auto makers.

In the *Teenager's Guide*, I told your sons and daughters that not all teachers are winners—that they get what they get. It's that simple. In many ways, this is a good life experience. Your sons and daughters will never have all great supervisors or bosses, either, and they should know that. The real test is to rise above the fray and make something good of the conditions as given.

Having a less-than-perfect teacher does not relieve students of responsibility to learn as much as they can from the class. It doesn't stop them from collaborating with other students to better learn the subject. It doesn't prevent them from trying to develop the teacher by getting the teacher involved. I point out that one way to do this is to approach the teacher as a group. They can tell her point-blank that they would like to have a great time learning her subject and that her cooperation would be appreciated.

You know this has never been done before. It's hard to imagine this happening. But is there any reason why learning should not be fun? I encourage you to talk with your student and ask what it would take to make school more fun and more rewarding. Stretch the envelope!

The Roles of Parents

You can do a lot to help your teens clarify their goals in life by explaining how you arrived where you are today, including your mistakes. Include the dreams you had, or didn't have.

Most of us, in our teens, did not have dreams that were based on solid assumptions. Neither do our children. The important thing is that we tell them that, so they don't go around like neurotics, thinking they are supposed to have clarified their life's work. This is the time to experiment, to imagine the possibilities, to create visions and to dream.

Don't overdo the presentation of your goals and dreams or try to excuse any past mistakes. State them simply, for the record. Teens, for the most part, think in terms of black and white, right or wrong. It will take some time and many more experiences for them to make enough mistakes and have to forgive themselves before they understand fully the road you've traveled.

An interesting phenomenon can happen during your time together. It may benefit you. As you review your life to-date, you will realize that you did have some dreams. In many ways those dreams may still be valid. There are things you had wanted to do, but never did, things you wanted to accomplish or become that now seem distant memories. As they start to revive, the passion and feelings that you felt then may engulf you, and you may find yourself wishing for the past. Consider bringing these passions to the present, like Gloria.

Gloria's Story

Gloria left high school early to follow and marry her Marine, the love of her life. She moved thousands of miles from her family to make a life with him. Life became hell for over thirty years. She endured spousal abuse, loneliness, and depression. Finally she amassed the strength to divorce.

With few skills, she could only get menial jobs, but she got by. With the modest settlement from the divorce, she was able to purchase a small bungalow. Life was tough, but she was free.

As a teen, her passion had been fashion design. With help from some friends, she rekindled the flame, designing specialty clothing for sale at craft shows throughout the region. Her designs and the quality of her work made her an instant success. In an arena where most

> Challenges make you discover things about yourself that you never really knew. They're what make the instrument stretch: what make you go beyond the norm.
>
> Cicely Tyson

> Fire is the test of gold, adversity of strong men.
>
> Seneca

> Every experience, however bitter, has its lesson, and to focus one's attention on the lesson helps one overcome the bitterness.
>
> Edward Howard Griggs

> Every new day begins with possibilities. It's up to us to fill it with the things that move us toward progress and peace.
>
> Ronald Reagan

> No yesterdays are ever wasted for those who give themselves to today.
>
> Benjamin Franklin

things look alike, she stood out. Today, she earns thousands of dollars a week end during the summer. She rejoices at the new levels of self confidence she has gained from the unconditional acceptance of others.

Inside each of us is a cluster of talents that are unique to us. Within this cluster lies an energy field of passion and happiness that only we can bring out, if we choose. Doing so creates not only a new story, a new song or a new invention, it also creates anew the person that unleashes it. Anthony Robbins, was near rock bottom in his life before turning things around to become a sought after motivational speaker and author.

It doesn't matter when you find your passion, so long as you take action when you do. Colonel Sanders was retirement age when he set off against the odds to create Kentucky Fried Chicken. Steve Jobs (Apple) and Bill Gates (Microsoft) found their paths much earlier in their respective lives.

If your dreams evoke in you the power and passion that they once did, consider how much fun they might be to have back in your life. If you were a budding writer, why not try it once again? Maybe you want to create a peaceful garden and achieve some level of balance away from your work that refreshes you. You know what you loved and were good at. Do it. As you proceed down this road, you'll have to drop some old habits.

You may have to forego television or your nap on the couch but these are small prices to pay for a new you. Commit to make whatever changes you have to.

If you elect to take this road to rediscovery and revitalization, be prepared for a second phenomenon. You'll gain newfound respect from your children. They'll see a new person evolving, one who is happier and more energetic. They'll also have a new role model to emulate. You'll be demonstrating, by example, that they should think seriously about their passions and how they can follow them. They'll start earlier in their pursuits. Hopefully their lives will be as enriched as your new life will be.

> Each day is a new life. Seize it. Live it.
>
> David Guy Powers

1. Will & Ariel Durant, *The Lessons of History*, New York, Simon Schuster, p. 20

7 — Creating Your Life

We have come to the end of our time together. I wish we had more. I want to leave you with these thoughts from a father of two, who loves his sons, both for who they are and for what they are.

For the first few years of their lives, much of what they did, they did together. Both were in soccer leagues, although on different teams. Both learned karate and earned their first black belts from the same instructor. Both went into the Boy Scouts, Aaron following in his brother's path a year or so after Chris.

As they grew older, their individual interests pulled them toward differing paths. Chris stuck with karate and the Boy Scouts, earning his eagle scout status. He added marching band in seventh grade and stayed with it throughout his high school years. His band took state honors in his junior year. Aaron left the scouts after two years and lost interest in karate after achieving his black belt. He became involved with tennis and mountain biking and joined the high school theater as plays as fly captain (stage setting),

Chris received his Bachelor of Arts in biology with honors after five years at Oakland University. During this time he became more heavily involved in martial arts, linking up with such notables as Guro Dan Inosanto and Salem Assili. If you're into martial arts, you understand the significance of these associations. Chris has established a following in Michigan and opened his own kwoon (martial arts academy) to teach a number of martial arts. This is what he wants to do with his life. He will be successful at it and earn a much better than average income.

Aaron is completing his bachelor's degree with a double major in Communications and French at Oakland University. He will go on for a masters degree in counseling. Much of his recent life has revolved around university life. He is an officer in the Sigma Pi Fraternity, and served for a time in student congress. Both boys have chosen different paths. Neither has elected to follow his father's path. So it should be.

In his book, **The Prophet,** author and philosopher Kahlil Gibran wrote about children through his character, Almustafa:

And a woman who held a babe against her
bosom said,
"Speak to us of Children."
And he said:
Your children are not your children.
They are the sons and daughters of Life's
longing for itself.
They come through you but not from you,
And though they are with you, yet they
belong not to you.
You may give them your love but not your
thoughts.
For they have their own thoughts.
You may house their bodies but not their
souls,
For their souls dwell in the house of
tomorrow, which you
cannot visit, not even in your dreams.
You may strive to be like them, but seek not
to make them like you.
For life goes not backward nor tarries with
yesterday.
You are the bows from which your children
as living arrows are sent forth.
The archer sees the mark upon the path of
the infinite, and He bends you with His
might that His arrows may go swift and far.
Let your bending in the archer's hand be for
gladness;
For even as he loves the arrow that flies, so
He loves also
the bow that is stable.

In our time together, Lynn and I gave our boys love and stability, structure and discipline, and a sense of the wonderful possibilities in life. We did not give them many material possessions, though what we did give them was substantial. What we did give them was more intangible: love, insight, discipline, ears that listened and heard, guidance, support, expectations, encouragement, and praise. We were open about things like family finances, developing personal values and personal responsibility. We shared their thoughts with them when they wanted, and gave guidance when asked.

For their part, Chris and Aaron are creating lives of their own choosing, aware that life is finite and fleeting. Each will make his mark based on his individual commitment to a personal dream.

I'm sure as each son starts his own family, he will think about what he learned while with us. He will keep what is important and discard the rest. Chris might remember that I didn't camp out with him and his scouts as often as other dads. That was important to him, and I let him down. For a young boy with numerous peers, it was hard. Aaron's regrets are that, though we are close, he still doesn't know me as well as he'd like. He'd like us to spend a few days together to fill in the blanks - about my life and Lynn's —to" connect". We live in the same house, but we're leading our individual lives separately. Both boys will make sure that they don't repeat what they see as our mistakes.

Your teens will soon be selecting a path of their own. Help them choose carefully. They should learn all they can from their experiences, keeping what they deem important, discarding the rest. They should remember what hurt them and commit not do it to others, to forgive those who have wronged them, for those people might not have known any better. They must know that carrying negative feelings along will only weigh them down. They have far too many important things to do than to carry old baggage.

I leave you with the message I wrote for Chris upon his graduation from college.

With my best wishes that you achieve the life you choose as your teens achieve theirs,

To Christian....

I remember your high school graduation gathering with the family. I made a little speech and got teary eyed; Mother beamed with pride, water in her eyes as well. Tonight we are celebrating your graduation from college. I will once again raise a glass in your honor and, perhaps, once again weep tears of pride. As I reflect on all you've achieved in your life, I can't help but be proud. You have demonstrated laser-like focus on your goals and intensity, passion and perseverance in their pursuit. I am sure you will succeed in whatever you choose.

When you were born, if someone had told me that my son would become a leading martial artist, I would have scoffed. It never would have occurred to me to consider that end. But, as Kahlil Gibran had authored in <u>The Prophet</u>, parents are not placed on earth to decide how their children would live, but only to give them life. I had no predispositions for you other than the hope that you would be blessed with the vision to see your life's purpose and the good fortune to pursue it. Mom and I gave you a foundation of security, love, values, support and nurturing. We let your leanings take you where they would, so you could experience much and select from that what you wanted to keep, discarding the rest. You have, indeed, been blessed and you have acted to take advantage of what you know, in your heart, is your destiny.

I admonish you to consider that while the universe is endless and replete with opportunities, your time in it is finite. As you have learned from your relentless pursuit of knowledge in the martial arts, the secret is balance. Think about your own life's balance and the needs of others who love you. Somewhere, you should take the time to achieve balance, giving as well as taking, listening as well as speaking, thinking deeply as well as racing frantically. Think now about what you would want your legacy to be. Project yourself into the future, to the closing days of your life and imagine how you want to be remembered - and for what. With that in mind, point yourself in the direction of your dreams, set sail and don't look back.

upon his graduation from Oakland University, December 18, 1995

Appendix

Fastest growing occupations

Fastest growing industries

Industries with largest job growth

Reasons to go to college

Reasons why *not* to go to college

Reasons why people chose the college they did

College credits through CLEP

External Degree Programs

Median starting salaries of college grads, 1993

The military option

Recommended reading list

Fastest Growing Occupations 1994-2005
(in percent)

Personal and home health care aides*	119
Home health care aides	102
Systems analysts	92
Computer engineers	90
Physical and corrective therapy aide	83
Electronic pagination systems workers	83
Occupational therapy assistants and aides	82
Physical therapists	80
Residential counselors	76
Human services workers	75
Occupational therapists	72
Manicurists	69
Medical assistant	59
Paralegals	58
Medical records technicians	56
Teachers, special education	53
Amusement and recreation attendants	52
Corrections officers	51
Operations research analysts	50
Guards	48

Over half of these occupations are in the health or social services areas
Source: Bureau of Labor Statistics, *Occupational Outlook Quarterly*, Fall 1995
*Author's note: Categories in **Bold** may require specialized (vocational) or on-the-job training but do not require four year college degrees.

Fastest Growing Industries 1994-2005
(in percent)

Home health care services *	120
Residential care *	83
Miscellaneous business services *	79
Automotive Services, except repair	75
Computer and data processing services *	70
Individual and miscellaneous social services*	69
Offices of other health practitioners	65
Child day care services	59
Personnel supply services *	58
Services to buildings *	58
Miscellaneous equipment rental and leasing	51
Security and commodity exchanges and services	50
Management and public relations	47
Nursing and personal care services	46
Health and allied services not elsewhere classified	46
Miscellaneous personal services	45
Miscellaneous amusement and recreational services	44
Job training and related services	43
Museums and botanical and zoological gardens	42
Motion picture production and distribution	40

A large number of these fast growing industries (*) also account for the largest numerical increase in jobs.

Source: Bureau of Labor Statistics, *Occupational Outlook Quarterly*, Fall 1995

Industries With the Largest Job Growth 1994-2005
(in thousands of jobs)

Education, public and private	2,213
Personnel supply services	1,310
Miscellaneous business services	1,077
Eating and drinking places	1,020
Nursing and personal care facilities	751
Home health care services	665
Computer and data processing services	661
Grocery stores	593
Offices of physicians	566
Individual and miscellaneous social services	536
Residential care	498
Services to buildings	496
Hospitals, public and private	485
Miscellaneous amusement and recreational services	429
Local government except education and hospitals	369
Legal services	343
Management and public relations	333
Child day care services	298
Hotels and other lodging places	282
Miscellaneous shopping goods stores	271

Top 8 will account for half the growth in wage and salary jobs.
The top 20 will account for nearly 80 percent of the growth in wage and salary jobs. The Bureau of Labor Statistics projection models are made up of 260 industries.
Source: Bureau of Labor Statistics, *Occupational Outlook Quarterly*, Fall 1995

Reasons to Go to College

You want to

College grads earn more money during their working career (about $700,000 more) than those without college degrees

College grads get better jobs

You really like the academic life

It is necessary to get into the field you want

You want the intellectual challenge

Your folks want you to

Everyone in your school goes on to college

You want the "college experience"

Reasons *Not* to Go to College

You have no interest in academic subjects

Other interests are more important to you

You don't have the money

You're not ready to tackle the responsibilities

You want to get a job instead

You want to travel

Your parents want you to

Everybody in your school goes on to college

Vocational training is faster and more meaningful

You have more immediate concerns

It doesn't mesh with the way you see yourself

You are not prepared emotionally or mentally

Why People Chose the College They Did

It was close to home
It was *far* from home

It was what they could afford
They received a scholarship
The college had the best financial aid package

The school is a recognized leader in their chosen field
The curriculum met their educational needs
The school's reputation
To network with others
Status
To associate with the best and the brightest
They liked the challenging environment
Ratio of professors to students
Size of student body
Ratio of women to men

It was consistent with their self-image
Their closest friend was going there
Their parents went there

It is Ivy league

The environment is not too taxing
Entrance requirements were loose
It's a great party school
It has great sports teams
The climate suited them

College Credits Through CLEP

The College Level Examination Program (CLEP) was designed to help people shorten the time to get a degree by allowing them to *test out* of subjects they already know well enough to pass. For example, let's say you really like art and humanities and read a lot about them on your own. If you were given a comprehensive final exam on the broad elements of the subject, you are confident you would pass it. Then, the CLEP has a test for you.

You can sign up for a CLEP test at any local college that gives it (usually, any college will administer the tests once a month). The fee is somewhere in the range of $42 - $55. If you pass the test, you have earned college credit for the course (usually 3-4 credits, depending on the college). In effect you've reduced the time by some fifteen weeks and saved as much as $350 in the process.

To find out more, visit your local library or bookstore and ask for the books on the CLEP. The CLEP manual includes outlines of each type of course— Math, English, Economics, Humanities— and recommended readings to bring up your level of proficiency. It even includes sample exams for each subject, so you can test your current knowledge against the standards. If you get a score above 50 percent on the sample test, I would suggest you take the test.

External Degree Programs

You might think of these as colleges without walls, whereby it is up to you as the student to learn the subjects on your own, take the tests, and get the grades— all outside of a traditional college setting. External degree programs are great if you travel a lot, or relocate with a job and can't transfer your college credits to a college in the area. Understand that colleges are businesses, too, and they have restrictions on what they'll accept from outside schools.

Be wary of the college you choose. Make sure their degrees are accepted by major universities as the basis for your next degree. I know, for example, that a degree from Charter Oak State College, a State of Connecticut external degree program, is accepted at colleges all over the country, including Yale. Other programs have acceptance only within the school you're attending, so you are then "locked in" when you want to pursue a masters or a Ph.D. There is an excellent book listed in the appendix that lists 100 accredited colleges and universities (*College Degrees by Mail*).

External degree programs may not be the right vehicle for you because you want the college experience and the benefits that come from it, including the following:
- The fun of being in an academic environment, where learning involves interacting with others, and being exposed to great teachers and exciting courses.
- Socializing with students from all over the world, with diverse backgrounds.
- Support throughout the academic system to sustain you when you feel like cutting out, and tutoring from peers for your most difficult subjects.

You can only get those experiences by being there.

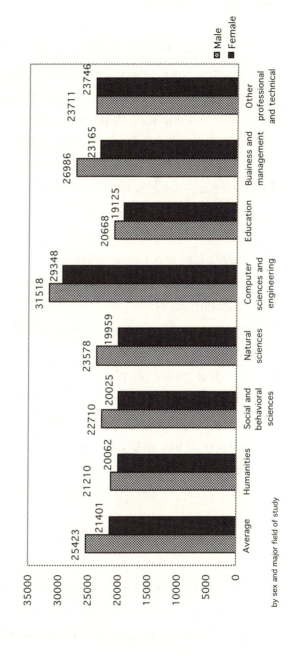

The Military Option

As a veteran of the U.S. military myself, I know the value of the military experience. What is written below is word-for-word what I told your teens. You may have a different opinion about the value of the service as an option. What is important, however, is that you and your son or daughter take the time to talk through all the issues.

There are many reasons for you to consider military service as a path after high school. Here are some:

- You want to serve your country.
- You see yourself as a leader and want to learn and develop leadership skills.
- You want to learn more about yourself by putting yourself in a challenging environment.
- You, like many people, like an ordered life. Military life is structured and disciplined. A soldier knows what is expected of him or her almost everyday of the enlistment.
- You would like to get a college degree, but can't afford it.
- You want to learn vocational skills that you can use in civilian life.

There's a lot to be said for a tour of duty in the military after high school, especially if you are not sure what it is you want to be. There's the travel. The U.S. military has bases all over the world. Imagine being stationed in Europe or Asia for a year. You get to meet a lot of new people and experience new cultures. You can even learn a new language. With thirty days vacation per year, you can plan exciting trips to other countries. I have friends who were stationed in Italy that spent parts of their vacations in France, Germany and the Swiss Alps. They loved it. Do you know how many years you will have to work in a civilian job before you get thirty days vacation a year?

There's the opportunity for personal growth. The military is a great place to learn life skills like discipline, responsibility, and leadership. Soldiers and sailors who are not a lot older than you are entrusted with a great deal of responsibility. They are charged with protecting the bases on which they're stationed or the ships they're aboard. They are given responsibility for millions of dollars in sophisticated, high-tech equipment.

If you are the one who has earned this trust, imagine how highly this reflects on you. You grow up fast in the military because it is *assumed* that you have what it takes to do the job. Think about that! You're a teen, yet you are treated like an adult, part of a team that is recognized the world over.

The military offers a wide variety of training programs to meet its needs. They range from the construction trades — plumbing, carpentry, electrical, and heavy equipment operation — to mechanics, medical and dental technicians, to hotel and restaurant management. Many high-tech electronics, engineering and programs in scientific disciplines are available to those who qualify. There is even training for reporters and photographers. There are over 125 training programs. Many of the courses also qualify for college credits.

If you want to get a college degree, the military offers a number of ways to get one. If you take college courses in your spare time while on active duty, the military will pay 75 percent of the tuition costs.

You can take courses at a college campus or by mail. Either is acceptable.

Another option is to join the Reserve Officers Training Corps (ROTC). There are a number of variations of ROTC programs, but they all cover tuition and pay a small allowance. There are specific minimum requirements for acceptance in ROTC programs.

Yet another route is the Montgomery GI Bill. In this program, $100 is deducted from your pay each month for the first twelve months of your enlistment. You will be eligible to receive at least $10,800 in educational benefits. At the time of this writing, the amount is $14,400. You will be eligible to use your benefits after two continuous years on active duty. These benefits expire ten years after your release from active duty. There is even a plan for reservists, called Selective Reserve Duty, that pays over $7,000 for college expenses. Any recruiter in any branch of the armed forces can tell you more about these programs when you're ready.

With all the emphasis the military places on training and education, the following statements might not seem necessary, but I think they are. Our whole world is changing as a result of rapid leaps in technology, from lasers to medicine or fiber optics. The military is being impacted as well. In many cases, it is in the forefront of change. This means that the caliber of people they enlist has to be as high as any civilian job. High tech weaponry needs people of skill to operate it. The military is as demanding of its people as any quality civilian employer. Whether you're looking for a tour or a career, be prepared to contribute to the fullest.

Consider enlisting in the military for what it can do for you. It will challenge you to be your best. You'll have the chance to become a leader. The military will train you for jobs you can do in civilian life. It will fund all or most of your college education should you decide you want one. You'll learn and be able to apply the lessons of discipline, responsibility and accountability, and leadership. In just a few short years you'll have a lot of achievements for your resume.

Employers look favorably on applicants who have had military service. They see them as candidates who have discipline and a strong work ethic. The twenty one or twenty two year old vet is perceived as better seasoned and more mature than a civilian of the same age. Most civilians have not had the breadth of life experience that a vet has.

Employers also value the quality of training the military gives its soldiers and sailors. They know that the schools have years of experience in turning out knowledgeable and capable men and women. They also know how valuable that experience is for their companies and will often pay a premium for it. They know a trained employee produces results faster than a trainee.

A tour of duty in the military can be a valuable experience for teens coming out of high school who are not yet prepared for a career. For many, it is an excellent way to make the transition to adulthood.

Recommended Reading List

Book	Author	ISBN#
Occupational Outlook Quarterly	Superintendent of Documents PO Box 371954 Pittsburgh, PA, 15250-7954	This is a subscription. Two years for $19
The Three Boxes of Life and How to Get Out of Them	Richard N. Bolles	0-913668-58-3
Do What You Love, the Money Will Follow	Marsha Sinetar	0-440-50610-1
Wishcraft - How to Get What You Really Want	Barbara Sher	345-34087-2
The Mainspring of Human Progress	Henry Grady Weaver	0-910614-02-4
Zen and the Art of Making A Living	Laurence G. Boldt	0-14-019469X

How to Write and Give a Speech	Joan Detz	0-312-08218-5
Presentations Plus	David A. Peoples	0-471-63103-5
Doing it Now	Edwin C. Bliss	0-553-27875-4
Study for Success	Meredith D. Gall, Ph. D	0-9305-3901-4
Skills for Success	Soundview Executive Book Summaries 5 Main St. Bristol, VT 05443	
How to Get Your Point Across in 30 Seconds or Less	Milo O. Frank	0-671-72752-4
The Wealthy Barber	David Chilton	0-7615-0166-5
Looking Beyond the Ivy League - Finding the College That's Right for You	Lauren Pope	0-14-02.39529
College Degrees by Mail	Bear & Bear	No ISBN# listed

The Work of Nations	Robert B. Reich	0-679-73615-8
Asserting Yourself	Sharon Anthony & Gordon H. Bower	0-201-57088-2
A Peacock in the Land of Penguins	Barbara Huteley Warren H. Schmidt	1-881052-71-0
Smart Questions	Dorothy Leeds	0-425-11132-6
Listening, the Forgotten Skill	Madelyn Burley-Allen	0-471-08776-9
Creative Visualization	Shakti Gawain	0-553-22689-4
Choices	Shad Helmstetter	0-671-67419-6
Finding the Fountain of Youth Inside Yourself	Shad Helmstetter	0-671-74620-0
The Art of Talking So That People Will Listen	Paul W. Swets	0-13047-837-7
How to Write and Give a Speech	Joan Detz	0-312-08218-5

The Index of Leading Cultural Indicators	William J. Bennett	0-671-88326-7
The Rubicon Dictionary of Positive, Motivational Life-Affirming & Inspirational Quotations	John Cook	0-9630359-3-2
The Lessons of History	Will & Ariel Durant	Library of Congress # 68-19949
cam report - career movement and management facts	Priam Publications, Inc. P.O. Box 1862 Lansing, MI 48826	

I have included ISBN #s or Library of Congress numbers for you because it is sometimes easier for a book store clerk to access a book using them instead of the name.

Order Form

**Imagine the Future - A Teenager's Guide to the
          Next Century - and Beyond** _____ copies
Imagine the Future - A Parents' Guide   _____ copies
                                                  _____ total

1-99	_____ copies @ $8.95 each	= $_____ total
100-999	_____ copies @ 8.25 each	= $_____ total
1,000-4,999	_____ copies @ 7.25 each	= $_____ total
5,000-9,999	_____ copies @ 6.25 each	= $_____ total
10,000 or more	_____ copies @ 4.95 each	= $_____ total

PLEASE SPECIFY WHICH BOOK(S) YOU WANT AND THE RESPECTIVE QUANTITIES

Name _____
Title _____
Organization _____
Street Address _____
City _____ State _____ ZIP _____
Phone( ) _____ FAX ( ) _____

Purchase Order# _____ (if applicable)

Check enclosed _____

Charge Account _____   Master Card _____ VISA

ACCOUNT NUMBER _____ EXP. _____

SIGNATURE _____

Applicable sales tax, shipping, and handling charges will be added. Prices effective March 1997 are subject to change. Orders payable in U.S. Dollars.

Career Solutions
P.O. Box 99455 Troy, MI 48089-9455   (810) 879-0681   FAX (810) 879-6936

Yes,

_____ Please send me information on Imagine the Future seminars for teens.

_____ Please send me information on training programs for teachers and administrators.

Name _____ Title _____
Address _____
City _____ State ____ ZIP _____

Specifically, I would like information on :

_____
_____
_____
_____
_____

Mail orders or inquiries to

Career Solutions   P.O. Box 99455   Troy, MI 48099-9455
Phone: (810) 879-0681 Fax: (810) 879-6936
e-mail: jmalgeri@detroit.freenet.org

Feel free to call, Fax or e-mail us with your thoughts, concerns or things you're doing that are working/not working. We'd love to hear from you.